wild, wild world

BIRDS OF PREY
AND OTHER FEATHERED FRIENDS

Written by
Denny Robson

Illustrated by
Sarah Lees

This is a Parragon Publishing Book
First published in 2001

Parragon Publishing
Queen Street House
4 Queen Street
Bath BA1 1HE, UK

Copyright © Parragon 2001

Produced by

David West ☗ Children's Books
7 Princeton Court
55 Felsham Road
Putney
London SW15 1AZ, UK

British Library Cataloguing-in-Publication Data

A catalogue record for this book is available from
the British Library.

ISBN 0-75254-685-6

Printed in Italy

Designers
Jenny Skelly
Aarti Parmar
Illustrator
Sarah Lees
(SGA)
Cartoonist
Peter Wilks
(SGA)
Editor
James Pickering
Consultant
Steve Parker

CONTENTS

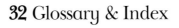

Which are the biggest birds?

The African ostrich can grow to over eight feet tall, which is much taller than the average man. The huge wandering albatross has the largest wingspan in the world, at nearly ten feet. Its long, pointed wings make it an excellent glider.

Ostrich

 Amazing! There are around 9,000 different kinds of birds, in many colors, shapes and sizes. They live all over world, in steamy jungles, icy regions, by the sea, in towns, and some move from one area to another when they migrate.

? Which are the smallest birds?

Rufous hummingbird

Hummingbirds are the smallest birds in world. The bee hummingbird of Cuba is no bigger than a bumblebee! Hummingbirds can flap their wings at up to 90 beats per second. They get their name from the humming sound their wings make.

Albatross

? What are birds?

Birds all have two legs, two wings, a beak, they lay eggs and they are the only animals that have feathers. But not all birds can fly, and not all flying animals are birds.

Is it true?
The first bird dates back to dinosaur times.

Black-faced ant thrush

Yes. Archaeopteryx is the earliest bird-like creature that we know of. It lived 150 million years ago. It had a head like a reptile, sharp teeth, a long tail and feathered wings.

Sparrowhawk

? What is a bird of prey?

Birds of prey catch and eat other animals. They are excellent hunters, with strong hooked beaks and sharp claws called talons, which they use to kill and tear at prey.

? Why are birds of prey good hunters?

The eyes of a bird of prey are different from other birds' eyes. They're very big, and face forwards so they can judge detail and distance well. A buzzard's eyes are as big as yours!

Buzzard

Amazing! Eagles can catch animals much bigger and heavier than themselves. The harpy eagle which lives in South American jungles is the biggest eagle of all. It has huge feet which it uses for grabbing and crushing monkeys and other animals.

Is it true?
Some birds eat eggs.

Yes. The Egyptian vulture uses stones to break into its favorite food, ostrich eggs. Birds can have very fussy tastes. Bat hawks, for example, only eat bats. Some eagles eat fish, while others prefer snakes.

How do ospreys hunt?
Ospreys fly high above the water looking for fish. When they spot one, they dive and enter the water feet-first to catch it. Their toes have tiny sharp spikes for gripping slippery fish.

Osprey

? Which bird is a national symbol?

Eagles are the most powerful birds of prey and are often pictured on flags. The bald eagle is the national emblem of the USA, standing for strength and power.

Is it true?
The peregrine falcon can travel faster than an express train.

Yes. When it spots a flying bird, the peregrine falcon folds its wings close to its body and dives at up to 220 mph.

Vultures

? Which birds are trash collectors?

Vultures wait for creatures to die before rushing down to eat everything except the bones. They are very useful birds, getting rid of dead animals before they rot and spread disease.

? Which birds can be trained?

Hawks and falcons can be trained by people. Hawks fly fast and low over the ground when they hunt. A long time ago the goshawk used to be trained to catch food for people. It was known as the cook's bird.

Peregrine falcon on falconer's glove

Amazing! The Andean condor from South America is the biggest bird of prey. It has a wingspan of over nine feet and it weighs up to 24 pounds.

Which owl is as white as snow?

The snowy owl lives in the icy Arctic. The male's feathers are pure white so that it can't be seen against the snow when it hunts for hares and lemmings. It has feathers on its feet to help keep its toes warm.

Snowy owl

Why do owls hoot?

Owls make sounds to communicate with each other in the dark. Different owls have different calls. They also use a wide range of sounds, from clicks to grunts to hisses. When courting, some owls actually sing to each other!

? How many types of owl are there?

There are 133 different kinds of owl, most of which hunt at night. Their special soft feathers mean they fly silently through the dark. With huge eyes and excellent hearing, they can swoop down to take prey by surprise.

Barn owl

Amazing! When an owl eats its prey there are usually parts it cannot digest, such as claws, teeth, beaks and fur. These parts are made into balls called pellets and passed back out through the bird's mouth.

Is it true?
An eagle owl's ears are on top of its head.

No. The tufts on top of its head may look like ears, but they are only long feathers. The owl's real ears are under the feathers at the sides of its head.

Eagle owl

? Why do birds have feathers?

Birds have three different kinds of feathers: down to keep warm; body feathers to cover and protect; and flight feathers. Baby birds have down feathers and can't fly until they've grown all their flight feathers.

Albatross chick

Is it true?
All flamingos are pink.

No. In the wild, flamingos are generally pink. Color from the food is absorbed and passes to the feathers. But in captivity, their feathers can turn white if they have a change of diet.

? How do birds keep clean?

All birds comb, or preen, their feathers with their beaks and claws. Love birds preen each other. Most birds also spread oil on their feathers from a gland above the tail, which keeps them waterproof.

Close-up of water on feathers

Tawny frogmouth and chick

❓ Why are some feathers bright and others dull?

Many woodland birds, such as the tawny frogmouth, have dull feathers so that they can blend in with their background and keep safe. Male birds are often more brightly colored to attract a mate.

13

Amazing! Most birds have over 1,000 feathers and some birds have an enormous number. Swans have about 25,000 feathers – more than almost any other bird!

How do birds fly?

Birds need to be light but strong to fly. They flap their wings to take off and fly higher in the air. As the wing flaps down, the flight feathers close against the air, which pushes the bird up and forward.

Reed warbler

14

What has to run to take off?

Swans are too big and heavy to leap into the air. Instead they have to run along the surface of the water, flapping their powerful wings to get enough speed to take off.

Swan

Amazing! Big seabirds glide on air currents, sometimes not landing for weeks. Other birds can stay in the air for months, while swifts can spend years in the air, only landing to nest and mate.

Kestrel

? What can fly and yet stay in the same spot?

Kestrels are experts at hovering. They fly into the wind and beat their wings very quickly. This lets them stay in the same position as they search for prey below.

Is it true?
Birds can only fly forwards.

No. Hummingbirds are special. They can fly forwards, sideways, backwards and hover on the spot by flapping their wings very quickly!

Pelican

? Whose beak can hold more than its stomach?

A pelican has a beak with a stretchy pouch which can hold far more fish than its stomach! It scoops fish from the water using its beak like a fishing net.

 Amazing! A woodpecker uses its unusual beak to drill for insects, to make holes in dying trees to use as nests, and to hammer on a tree to mark its territory.

? Why do birds have beaks?

Birds use their beaks to catch and hold food, to make nests and to preen themselves. They have different beaks because they eat different food. The toucan uses its enormous beak to pull fruits from delicate branches.

Toucan

Is it true?
Birds have teeth.

No. Birds cannot chew, so they grind food up with a gizzard inside their bodies, and sometimes by swallowing small stones too.

17

Yellow-headed parrot

? What climbs with its beak?

Parrots usually live in big noisy groups in tropical forests. They have short, curved powerful beaks for cracking nuts and seeds. Some parrots have beaks so strong that they can even use them to pull themselves up trees.

Why do ducks have webbed feet?

Water birds have skin between their toes. Their feet are like paddles, helping them move easily through the water. They can also walk on mud without sinking in.

African jacana

Amazing! Jacanas are water birds that live in tropical places. Their very long toes allow them to step on water plants without sinking. They are sometimes called "lily-trotters".

18

Redhead duck

Is it true?
Birds stand on one leg when they've hurt their foot.

No. When a bird stands on one leg, it is keeping the other foot warm, tucked up under its feathers.

? What has legs like stilts?

Herons and storks have very long legs which look like stilts. They are ideal for standing or wading in shallow water, where the birds use their long beaks to catch fish and frogs.

Heron

? Why don't birds fall when they sleep?

Birds have a long tendon attached to each toe. When they rest on branches or another perch, they bend their legs and their toes lock around the perch.

Budgerigar

? What hangs upside down to court?

When the male bird of paradise wants to attract a female it hangs upside down to show off its beautiful tail. Females and chicks are often dull compared to males so that they can remain safely hidden in the trees.

Male blue bird of paradise

 Amazing! Great crested grebes dance on the water in front of each other for several weeks before they finally mate and pair for life. They can perform four separate complicated dance routines.

? What hypnotizes with its "eyes"?

The male peacock has a fan made of beautiful jeweled feathers. The "eyes" on the feathers fascinate its mate, the peahen. By looking at them, she can tell that he is a healthy male to choose.

Peacock

 Is it true?
Birds stay with a mate for only one season.

No. Some birds, including swans, gannets and golden eagles, find a mate and stay with that same bird for the rest of their lives.

21

? What attracts its mate with a red balloon?

The male frigate bird has a bright red pouch under his chin. When he wants to find a mate, he puffs it out like a balloon. If the female is impressed, she rubs her head against the pouch.

Frigate birds

? Why do birds build nests?

Most birds build nests to hide their eggs and to keep their young warm and safe from enemies. Colonies of weaver birds often build several nests in the same tree.

Black-headed weaver birds

Hummingbird's nest

Amazing! Some nests are huge. An eagle's nest or eyrie is so big that you could lie down in it! Some birds, such as the hummingbird, make tiny nests. The bee hummingbird's nest is the same size as a thimble.

? Why do birds sit on their eggs?

Birds sit on their eggs to keep them warm while the baby birds inside grow. If the eggs get cold, the babies inside will die, so birds don't leave their eggs alone for long.

Thrushes

Is it true?
Nests are birds' homes where they sleep at night.

No. Birds only use nests for laying eggs and raising their chicks. They rest at night in hedges, trees or holes.

? Do birds' eggs all look the same?

Birds' eggs are often colored or patterned for camouflage. The guillemot's eggs are also an unusual shape. They are pointed at one end so that if nudged, they spin in a circle instead of rolling off a cliff.

? What do newly hatched birds look like?

The young of tree-nesting birds are naked and blind at first. Their parents have to look after them, and they are always hungry! They open their beaks wide and call loudly, which forces the parents to feed them.

Looking down on baby birds

Amazing! The hummingbird lays the world's smallest eggs. Each is only the size of your fingernail. Compared to this, an ostrich egg is huge, and thousands of times heavier.

Grebe with young

? What sits on its mother's back?

Baby grebes can swim soon after they hatch. When they get cold or tired, they sit on their mother's back to warm up and have a rest.

Which father sits on his eggs until they hatch?

The male ostrich makes eggs with up to twelve different females. The females all lay their eggs in the same nest. The male then sits on them himself until they hatch. Many types of male bird, including pigeons, take it in turns with the female to sit on the eggs.

Ostriches and chicks

Is it true?
A duckling could mistake you for its mother.

Yes. A duckling thinks that the first creature it sees after hatching is its mother. If you were around, that would be you!

25

? Which bird calls to find its nest?

When a male gannet has caught fish for his mate and young, he must call out and wait for the female's reply before he can find them amongst all the other gannets.

Gannets

? Why do birds sing?

Birds sing most of all during the breeding season. A male bird sings to attract a mate, or to tell other birds to keep away from his territory. Males and females also call to warn other birds that an enemy is near, such as a cat or a human.

Magpie-lark

Which birds copy sounds?

? Some birds are natural mimics. This means they can copy sounds, such as the telephone ringing or even human speech. The mynah bird used to be popular as a caged pet because of this talent. Australian lyrebirds can even imitate a chainsaw!

Amazing! The African gray parrot is a real chatterbox. It can learn up to 800 different words, but it doesn't know what they mean!

Superb lyrebird

Is it true?
Birds can sing very high notes.

Yes. Many birds can sing notes too high for us to hear! There is a wide range of beautiful birdsong, full of high and low notes.

Which bird finds its way home?

Pigeon

Pigeons have a great sense of direction. Scientists think they use the position of the Sun, Moon and stars, the Earth's magnetic pull and landmarks. People race pigeons as a hobby, because they usually find their way home safely.

Snow geese

Amazing! The arctic tern travels right across the Earth, from the Arctic to Antarctica and back again each year. That's a round trip of 22,000 miles. It keeps up its energy by eating fish as it flies.

Migrating birds must eat as they travel.

No. Many kinds of birds do not eat during their migration. Instead they eat large amounts of food before they leave in order to survive the trip.

? Which birds fly in a "V" pattern?

Geese migrate in groups like this, or they fly together in long chains. The younger birds learn which way to go by following the older birds in front.

29

? Do migrating birds remember the way?

Some migrating birds use familiar landmarks such as islands or mountains to find their way. Swifts often fly from the other side of the world back to the same nest each year.

Swift

? What was a dodo?

Have you heard the expression "as dead as a dodo"? Dodos were strange-looking, heavy birds that could not fly. They lived on islands in the Indian Ocean until sailors hunted the very last one. Sadly, they have been extinct since 1800.

Dodo

Kiwi

? What has invisible wings?

Kiwis are flightless birds whose wings are so tiny that you cannot see them. They have long whiskers, no tail and a good sense of smell. They hunt at night for worms and insects.

? Which bird "flies" underwater?

Penguins are water birds which cannot fly. They live in the chilly Antarctic. They slide on snow and ice using their bellies as toboggans. But in water they are very graceful, using their wings as flippers as they swim along catching fish.

Is it true?
Penguins argue with their wings.

Yes. Penguins live close together. When they squabble with each other, they flap their wings and jab their beaks to help make their point!

King penguins

Amazing! Ostriches cannot fly, but they can run very quickly indeed. The African ostrich can sprint along at 40 mph! They live in dry grasslands and may have to travel a long way for food.

Glossary

Camouflage Colors, shape or markings of a bird or animal that help it blend into its background so that it is hard to see.

Colony A large group of birds or animals all living together. Gannets are birds that live in colonies.

Falconer Someone who breeds and trains falcons and hawks.

Flock A large group of birds.

Gizzard A special second stomach that birds have, with strong muscles to help grind up and digest food.

Migrate To move from one place to another, often far away. Birds and animals may migrate to find warmer places to live each winter, or to find more food.

Mimicry When an animal or bird copies another. Some parrots and mynah birds can even mimic the sound of the telephone.

Predator An animal which hunts another animal for food.

Preening When a bird combs and tidies its feathers with its beak.

Prey An animal which is hunted for food.

Talons Long, curved claws. Birds of prey use their talons to grip and tear at their prey.

Tendon A strong cord which connects a muscle to a bone.

Territory An area of land where a bird or animal lives and finds food. Birds and animals defend their territories.

32

Index